CONTENTS

CHAPTER 1

A YOUNG GENIUS

In 1653, Isaac Newton lived in Grantham in Lincolnshire. He loved to read and experiment. He also had a talent for building machines. When he was 11 years old, he built a model of a mill.

Moving water can turn a wheel. The moving wheel provides energy to power the mill.

GRAPHIC LIBRARY™

INVENTIONS AND DISCOVERY

ISAAC NEWTON AND THE LAWS of MOTION

Andrea Gianopoulos

illustrated by Phil Miller
and Charles Barnett

Raintree

www.raintreepublishers.co.uk
Visit our website to find out
more information about
Raintree books.

To order:
☎ Phone 0845 6044371
🖨 Fax +44 (0) 1865 312263
✉ Email myorders@raintreepublishers.co.uk

Customers from outside the UK please telephone +44 1865 312262

Raintree is an imprint of Capstone Global Library Limited, a company incorporated in England
and Wales having its registered office at 7 Pilgrim Street, London, EC4V 6LB – Registered
company number: 6695582

Design: Alison Thiele
Colourist: Otha Zackariah Edward Lohse
UK editor: Diyan Leake
Originated by Capstone Global Library Ltd
Printed in China by South China Printing Company Ltd

ISBN 978 1 406 21569 4 (hardback)   ISBN 978 1 406 21574 8 (paperback)
14 13 12 11 10   15 14 13 12 11
10 9 8 7 6 5 4 3 2 1   10 9 8 7 6 5 4 3 2 1

British Library Cataloguing in Publication Data
Gianopoulos, Andrea -- Isaac Newton and the laws of motion
A full catalogue record for this book is available from the British Library.

Every effort has been made to contact copyright holders of material reproduced in this book. Any
omissions will be rectified in subsequent printings if notice is given to the publisher.

Disclaimer
All the Internet addresses (URLs) given in this book were valid at the time of going to press.
However, due to the dynamic nature of the Internet, some addresses may have changed, or sites
may have changed or ceased to exist since publication. While the author and publisher regret any
inconvenience this may cause readers, no responsibility for any such changes can be accepted by
either the author or the publisher.

Editor's note: Direct quotations from primary sources are indicated by a yellow background.

Direct quotations appear on the following pages:
Pages 13, 26, quoted in *Never at Rest: A Biography of Isaac Newton* by Richard S. Westfall
(Cambridge University Press, 1980).
Page 13 (paper), from *The Principia* by Isaac Newton, as quoted in *On the Shoulders of
Giants: The Great Works of Physics and Astronomy*, edited by Stephen Hawking
(Philadelphia: Running Press, 2002).

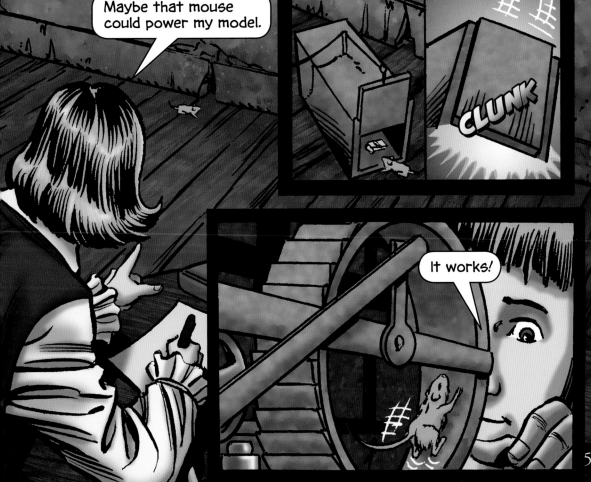

CHAPTER 2

BIRTH of a MASTERPIECE

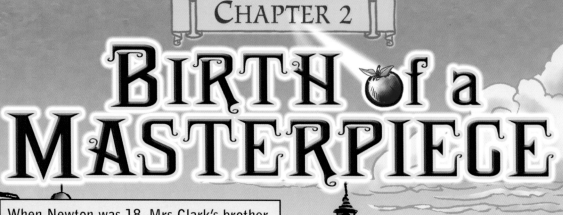

When Newton was 18, Mrs Clark's brother, Humphrey Babington, helped Newton enroll at Trinity College in Cambridge.

You'll have to work to help pay your expenses, Isaac.

I am grateful for the chance to be here at Trinity.

Your job will involve doing menial tasks for students and teachers alike.

Newton, are you finished polishing my buckles?

Not yet.

I wish I could be left alone to read without having to do these foolish tasks.

8

In the summer of 1665, the Great Plague hit Cambridge. The disease spread quickly by fleas that lived on rats. In England, the plague took many thousands of lives.

Trinity is closing to reduce the spread of the plague.

Where will you go, Isaac?

I suppose back to my family's farm at Woolsthorpe.

Trinity remained closed for two years.

At Woolsthorpe, Newton spent his days wondering how the universe worked and inventing the mathematics to describe it.

What keeps the Moon in orbit around the Earth? It must be a strong force to keep it moving so regularly. And this force must extend far from the Earth.

Newton couldn't find his equations. He promised to redo them. He sent his work to Halley three months later.

There is more work to be done on the forces that cause motion.

I've just read your proof. You should publish it.

Now that I am upon this subject, I would gladly know the bottom of it before I publish my papers.

Newton spent the next 18 months working day and night. Like in his college days, he often forgot to eat and slept only a few hours a night.

An object will remain at rest or in motion in a straight line unless acted upon by some force.

Every body preserves in its state of rest, or of uniform motion in a right line, unless it is compelled to change that state by forces impressed thereon.

The result of all this hard work was a book that came to be known as *The Principia.* This book forever changed how people view the world.

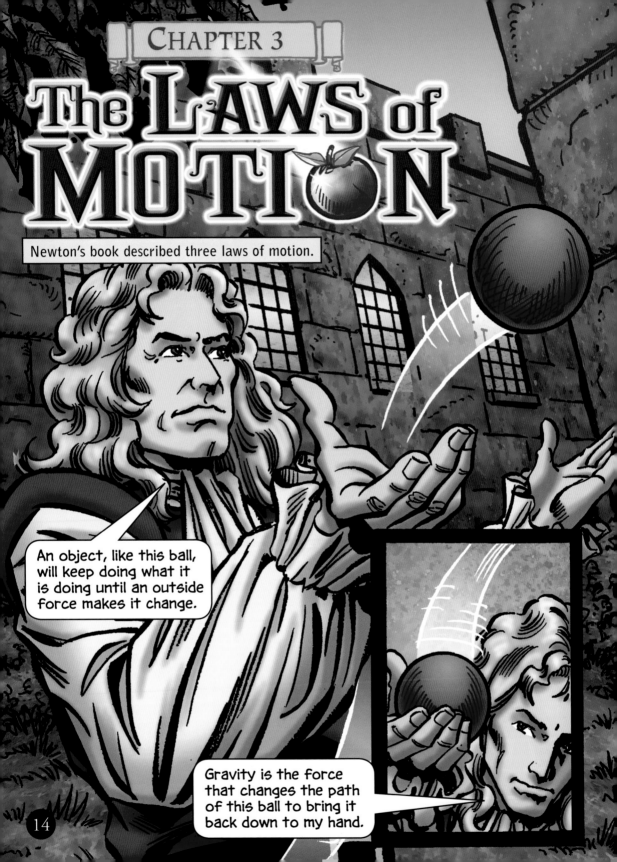

The object's motion depends on the strength of the force and the mass of the object.

If you kick a ball, it moves in the direction you kicked it. The force on the ball depends on how hard you kick it. The harder the kick, the faster the ball speeds up.

If you kick a ball that has more mass with the same force, the ball doesn't speed up as fast as the less massive ball.

Newton's third law of motion says that forces always come in pairs. When one object exerts a force on a second object, the second object exerts an equal and opposite force back on the first object. In other words, when you push on something it pushes you back.

When a bird flies, its wings push air down. The air reacts by pushing the bird up. The size of the force on the air equals the size of the force on the bird. And the forces are in opposite directions.

This law works on the water too.

Someone rowing a boat pushes water in the opposite direction of travel. The water pushes back on the oars with the same force, causing the boat to move.

When jumping from the boat to the dock, the legs push the body forward. The boat then pushes back in an equal and opposite direction. This force pushes the boat away from the dock.

Whoa!

21

Fired at a low velocity, it would travel in a straight line unless some force acted on it. That force is gravity. It pulls the cannonball back to Earth. That's the first law of motion at work.

A cannonball fired with a higher velocity would travel further before hitting the ground.

If the cannonball were fired at the right velocity, it would orbit the Earth. The cannonball would try to travel in a straight line out into space. But the force of gravity would tug at the cannonball and keep it going in a circle.

The balance between the force of gravity and an object's tendency to go straight would keep it in orbit.

23

CHAPTER 4

NEWTON'S LEGACY

The Moon's motion must be like that of the cannonball. So gravity affects motions on Earth and in space.

Newton's law of gravity explains that the Moon's gravity pulls a bulge of water toward it. It also pulls the Earth away from the water on the other side of the Earth. As the Moon orbits the Earth, the bulges get pulled along. The tides rise and fall depending on where these water bulges are.

HIGH TIDE

LOW TIDE

Although discovered more than 300 years ago, Isaac Newton's laws of motion still help scientists calculate orbits and send spacecraft to other planets.

ISAAC NEWTON

🍅 **Newton's Laws of Motion**
1st Law: An object will stay at rest or in motion in a straight line until some force acts on it.

2nd Law: The rate of change in velocity of an object depends on the object's mass and on the force acting on that object.

3rd Law: Forces come in pairs. When one object pushes on another object, that second object pushes back on the first object with a force of the same strength.

🍅 Isaac Newton was born on 25 December 1642. He died on 20 March 1727.

🍅 Newton designed and built a new type of telescope. The Newtonian reflecting telescope uses mirrors instead of lenses to bring light from distant objects into focus. Astronomers still use this type of telescope.

🍅 To explain his laws of motion, Newton invented a new kind of maths called calculus. Calculus lets you find the length, area, and volume of objects. It also lets you calculate how an object's position and velocity can change with time.

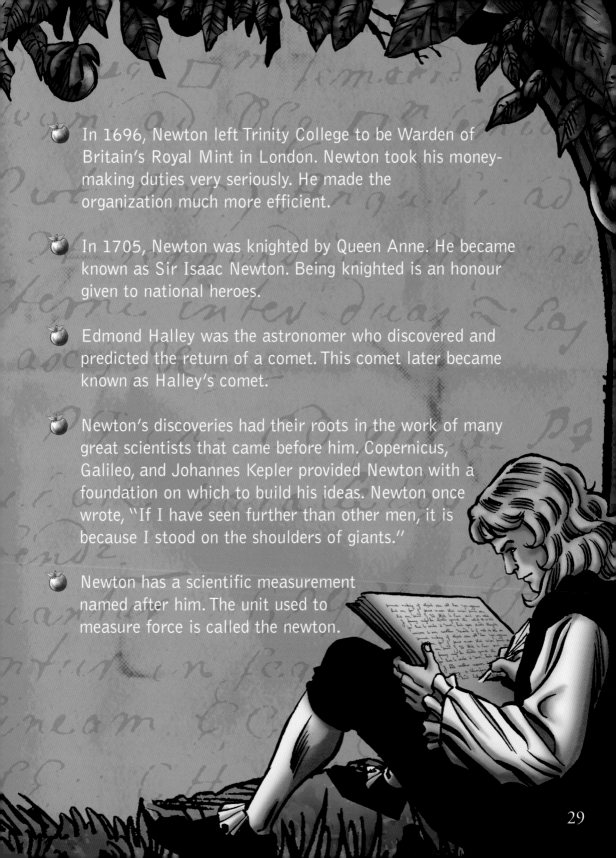

In 1696, Newton left Trinity College to be Warden of Britain's Royal Mint in London. Newton took his money-making duties very seriously. He made the organization much more efficient.

In 1705, Newton was knighted by Queen Anne. He became known as Sir Isaac Newton. Being knighted is an honour given to national heroes.

Edmond Halley was the astronomer who discovered and predicted the return of a comet. This comet later became known as Halley's comet.

Newton's discoveries had their roots in the work of many great scientists that came before him. Copernicus, Galileo, and Johannes Kepler provided Newton with a foundation on which to build his ideas. Newton once wrote, "If I have seen further than other men, it is because I stood on the shoulders of giants."

Newton has a scientific measurement named after him. The unit used to measure force is called the newton.

GLOSSARY

equation a mathematical statement, such as 5 x 3 = 15, or $3x + 2 = 14$

experiment test a scientific idea to see its effect

force action that changes the movement of an object

gravity force that attracts, or pulls, things together

mass amount of matter an object has

orbit path an object follows as it goes around the Sun or a planet

velocity measurement of both the speed and direction an object is moving

weight measure of how heavy a person or object is

INTERNET SITES

http://home.howstuffworks.com/science_projects_for_kids_laws_of_gravity_and_motion.htm

Find gravity-related science experiments on these web pages.

http://www.bbc.co.uk/history/historic_figures/newton_isaac.shtml

This web page provides a biography of Sir Isaac Newton.

MORE BOOKS TO READ

10 Experiments Your Teacher Never Told You About: Gravity, Andrew Solway (Raintree, 2005)

The Extreme Zone: Forces and Motion, Paul Mason (Raintree, 2006)

Isaac Newton (Giants of Science series), Kathleen Krull (Puffin, 2008)

Isaac Newton (Great Lives series), Philip Steele (QED Publishing, 2007)

Roller Coaster!: Motion and Acceleration, Paul Mason (Raintree, 2007)

The Story Behind Gravity (True Stories series), Sean Stewart Price (Heinemann Library, 2009)

FIND OUT MORE

Visit the house where Isaac Newton was born, and see the apple tree that inspired him in his study of gravity.

Woolsthorpe Manor
Water Lane, Woolsthorpe by Colsterworth, nr Grantham
Lincolnshire NG33 5PD
Telephone: 01476 860338
http://www.nhm.ac.uk/visit-us/darwin-centre-visitors/index.html

See the memorial where Isaac Newton was buried.

Westminster Abbey
20 Dean's Yard
London SW1P 3PA
Telephone: 0207 222 5152
http://www.westminster-abbey.org/our-history/people/sir-isaac-newton

INDEX